Fashion Coloring Bc

Copyright © 2016 Sephera Abigail

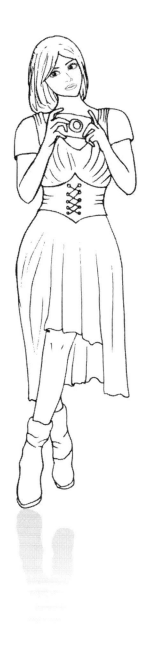  

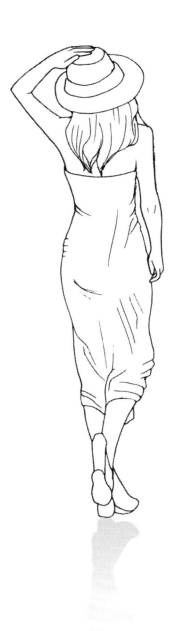

Trendy girls

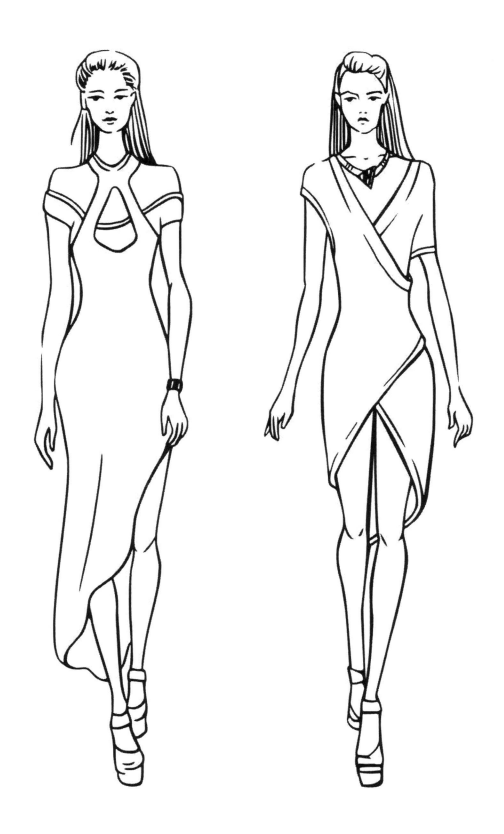

Thank you so much again for buying this book! I hope you enjoyed coloring my book. Now I'd like ask for a *small* favor. Could you please take a minute or two and leave a review for this book Amazon. It'd be greatly appreciated! And I truly value your opinion and thoughts and I will incorporate them into my next book, which is already underway.

Made in the USA
San Bernardino, CA
21 June 2017